Cherry Blossoms

General Awareness

UKG

FS3

SERIES EDITOR: RANI THIPPAVAZZULA

Preface

Cherry Blossoms provides graded, age-appropriate learning opportunities targeting holistic skill development for children in the age group of 3 years to 8 years. The series aligns with the vision outlined in the National Education Policy, 2020 for early years. It spreads across five levels, Nursery (Foundational Stage 1) to Class 2 (Foundational Stage 5). The books use a combination of hands-on activities, frequent recapitulation and child-friendly artwork to facilitate learning.

The series comprises **40 books** and spans **English**, **Maths**, **General Awareness**, and **Art and Craft**. The series comes bundled with a **workbook** for each subject and a book of **rhymes** and **stories** for Foundational Stage 1 to 3.

This series integrates the essence of **NIPUN Bharat** guidelines, which extensively deal with Foundational Literacy and Numeracy. The series aims to motivate learners to read independently, to improve their vocabulary, number sense and spatial understanding. The **Foundational Literacy and Numeracy (FLN)** skills include the skills for developing their critical thinking, logical reasoning and creative skills, as well as the skills to enhance their ability to express themselves both verbally and in writing.

Cherry Blossoms Teacher Support Materials include:

Teacher's Resource Books: Comprises stories, activity banks, classroom management and assessment guidelines

Multimedia eBook: Consists of animations, audio, video, slide shows, and interactive exercises

Print-ready Worksheets: Additional worksheets for practice and reinforcement, present in the digital support

Digital Flashcards: Flashcards with embedded sounds and animations for letter formation and letter-sound association

Animations and Songs: Animated stories and rhymes set to tune

Interactive Games: Interactivities to reinforce concepts in a fun and engaging manner

A note on the activity banks (included in the Teacher's Manuals)

The activity banks comprise hands-on activities that will help children develop the requisite skills to attain age-appropriate learning goals. In keeping with Howard Gardener's theory of multiple intelligences, the activity banks include options and variations that enable teachers to provide a planned cycle of experiences and opportunities, which foster each type of intelligence, to every child in their classrooms. The activity banks equip teachers to use the strengths of children as a means of complementing their less developed areas by valuing and nurturing the inherent abilities of the children.

Rani Thippavazzula, former Academic Director, Ravindra Bharathi Group is an eminent educationist with over two decades of experience in teaching, administration and curriculum design and development. As an Academic Advisor for chain schools pan India, she is proficient in developing learning products and is a specialist in Differentiated Instruction, Enterprise Education and Early Childhood Education.

Learning and Development During the Early Years

The early years are the most significant years for growth, development and learning. During this period, children need adequate opportunities for stimulating experiences as these favourably affect various learning abilities. Learning experiences, when chosen and planned properly, fuel the innate curiosity of children, and stimulate their thought processes.

The goal of learning during the early years is to enhance the all-round development of personality and to inculcate healthy attitudes, life skills and good values. Creative play, well thought-out games and developmentally appropriate activities help children develop the necessary skills to achieve these goals. The skills that children need to acquire can broadly be categorized as:

Motor:
Motor skills pertain not only to gross motor activities like walking and jumping but also include fine motor activities like the ability to hold a pencil and write. The development of motor skills is facilitated through several graded activities.

Personal, Social and Emotional:
Personal, social and emotional development, necessary for the overall personality development of children, is achieved using a combination of hands-on activities, role plays and thought-provoking stories and rhymes.

Linguistic:
The ability to listen, speak, read and write is critical to success in formal learning environments.

Mathematical:
The development of mathematical ideas and concepts is important at this stage since children will continue to build on this learning for most of their years of schooling.

Knowledge and Understanding of the World:
This is achieved through activities that enable children to explore their surroundings at home and in the school, and interact with the people that they see around them.

Health and Safety: The idea of health and safety is introduced through activities, stories and retelling of real-life experiences to encourage children to focus on health and well-being.

Creative:
Creative skills are developed through a host of activities involving art, craft, painting, roleplays, etc.

Logical and Rational Thinking:
Activities that involve simple puzzles, pattern-completion and visual discrimination help children to develop logical and rational thinking skills.

Contents

WALKTHROUGH

Short rhymes, set to tune, used to introduce fact-based concepts to facilitate recall. Follow-up practice exercises help reinforce the concept learnt

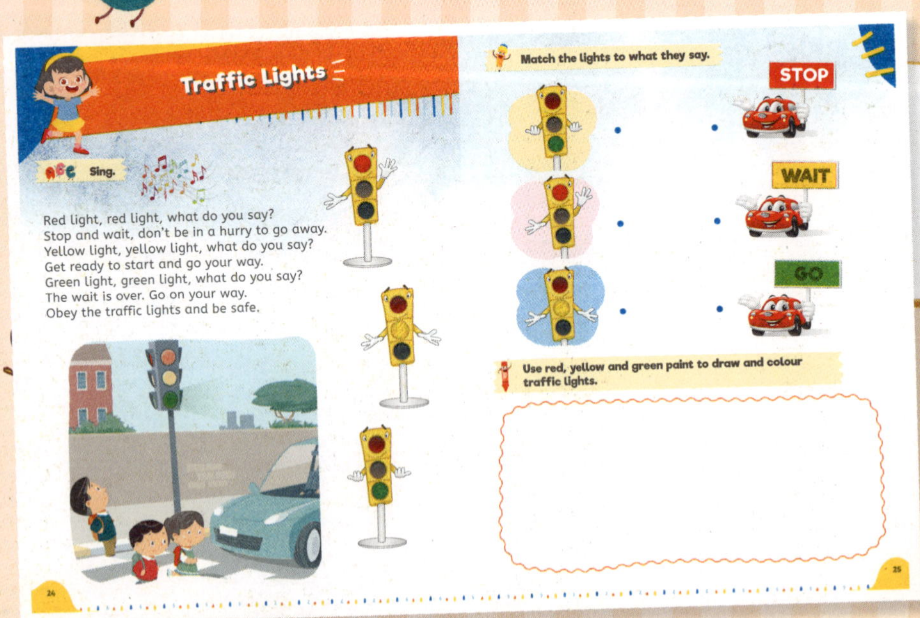

Varied revision activity formats to ensure holistic skill development

Revision activities such as these enable teachers to assess level of learning and recall without a formal assessment

Stories included to provide opportunities for activities and discussions that support social and emotional development

Full-page illustrations to depict real-world situations. The use of complete sceneries enables teachers to go beyond the immediate concept and engage students in activities, discussions, etc. to explore a topic in more details for enjoyable, discovery—based learning.

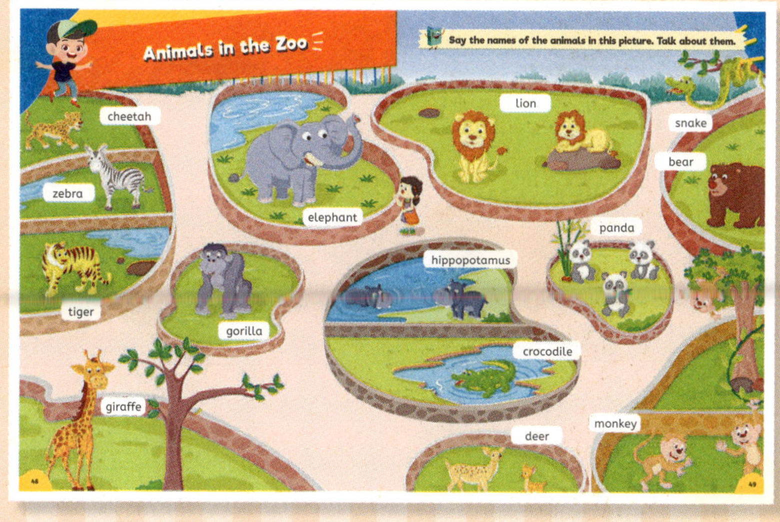

Keeping Clean and Staying Healthy

Tick (✓) the things you do to keep clean and stay healthy.

Can you help Petty take a bath? Tick (✓) the things he needs.

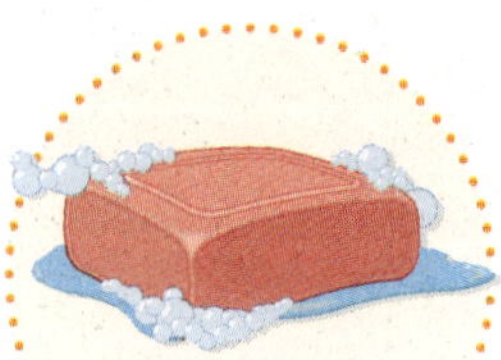

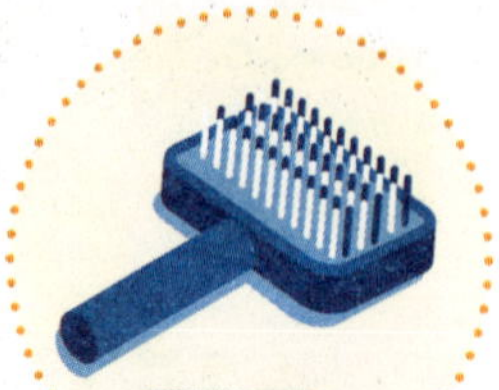

My Clean World

Ring the things you use to clean your teeth.

Draw the things that you use to keep clean.

Sense Organs

Read about the sense organs.

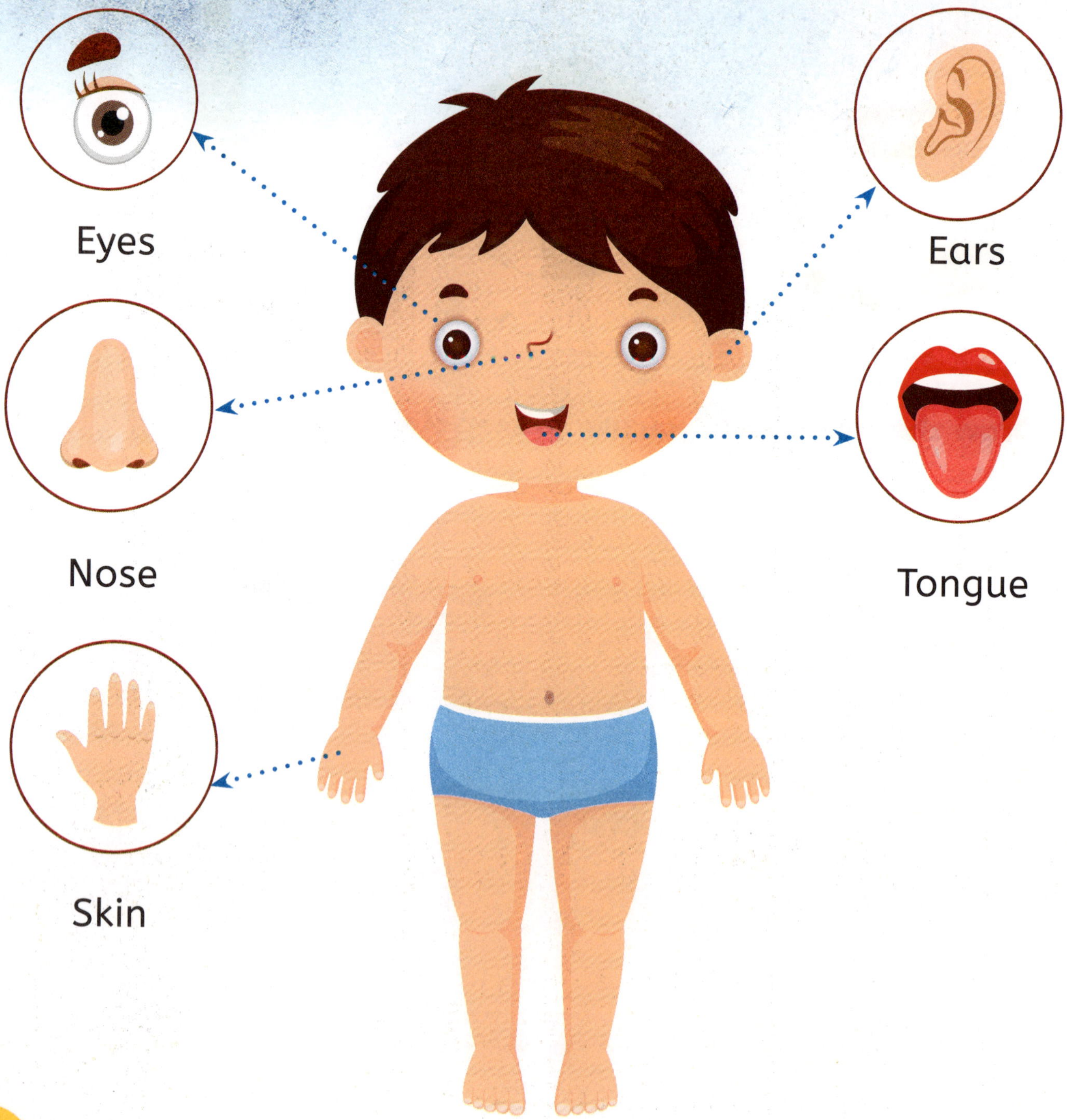

Match the organs to their use.

eyes • •

ears • •

nose • •

tongue • •

skin • •

Greetings

Sing.

When you get up and see
the sun bright,
wish good morning!

When you see the clock's hands
meet at noon, wish good afternoon!

When you see the sun setting,
wish good evening!

When it is dark and the moon
is bright, wish good night!

Match the pictures to the greetings.

Good morning!

Good afternoon!

Good evening!

Good night!

Tick (✓) the things you do in the morning.

Community Helpers

Read about the people who help us.

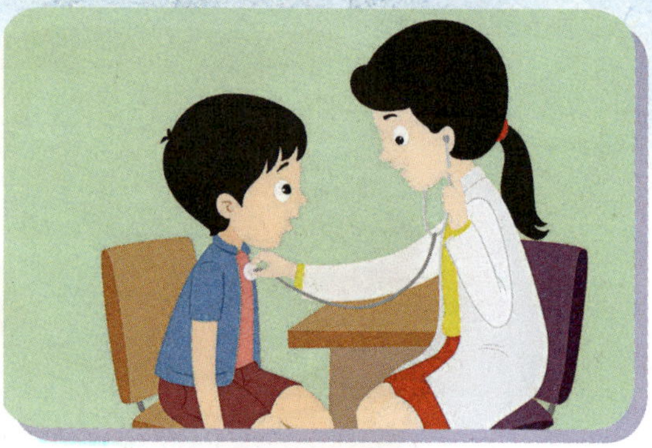

doctor

teacher

policeman

grocer

cobbler

postman

nurse

tailor

Match the correct pictures.

 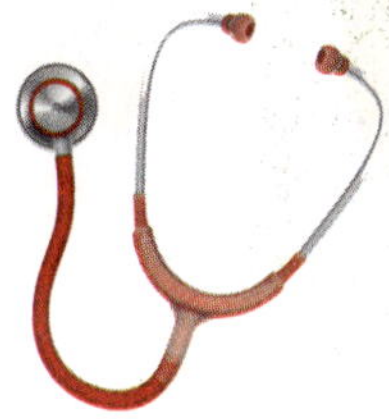

Meet More Colours

Meet the colour purple.

cabbage

crayon

eggplant

grapes

ink

Meet the colour brown.

potato

chocolate

crayon

monkey

bear

bread

violin

Colour the flowers purple.

Join the dots. Colour the picture brown.

Meet the colour pink.

rose

crayon

flamingo

Meet the colour orange.

orange

crayon

goldfish

orange drink

carrot

Match and make pairs.

Colour the unicorn's tail. Use colours purple, brown, pink and orange.

Fruits and Vegetables

Fruits

pear

papaya

strawberry

apple

banana

mango

orange

pineapple

watermelon

Vegetables

broccoli

carrot

turnip

beetroot

potato

radish

okra

cauliflower

capsicum

pumpkin

eggplant/brinjal

Take the fruits to the glass to make fruit juice.

orange

apple

papaya

carrot

beetroot

okra

pineapple

broccoli

pear

strawberry

Draw and colour fruits and vegetables to match the given colours.

Traffic Lights

Sing.

Red light, red light, what do you say?
Stop and wait, don't be in a hurry to go away.
Yellow light, yellow light, what do you say?
Get ready to start and go your way.
Green light, green light, what do you say?
The wait is over. Go on your way.
Obey the traffic lights and be safe.

Match the lights to what they say.

Use red, yellow and green paint to draw and colour traffic lights.

Safety at Home

Point and read.

I do not touch electrical appliances.

I do not play with sharp objects.

I do not jump on the bed.

I do not touch hot things.

I do not open the door
for any stranger.

Safety at School

Point and read.

I do not run on the stairs.

I do not push anybody.

I do not climb on the school desk.

I do not stand in a moving bus.

I do not shout.

Safety on the Road

Point and read.

I always walk with my elders.

I do not talk to strangers.

I never cross the road alone.

I always walk on the footpath.

I never put my head out of a moving vehicle.

Seasons

Point and read.

winter

summer

spring

rainy

Talk about the pictures.

summer

spring

rainy

winter

Paste stickers to show what you do in each season.

summer

winter

spring

rainy

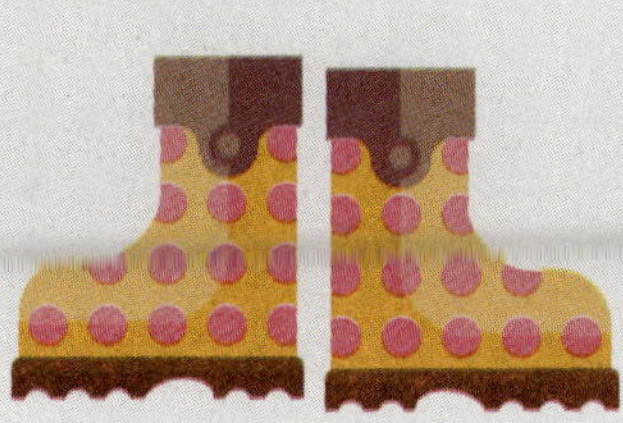

The Clothes We Wear

Point and read.

summer

t-shirt

shorts

frock

sunglasses

cap

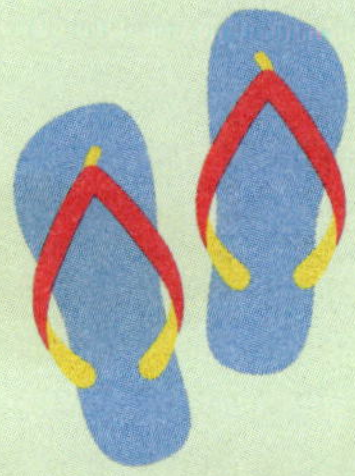

flip flops

rainy

raincoat

gumboots

umbrella

Point and read.

Draw two things we use in each season.

summer

rainy

winter

Identify the seasons. Talk about the differences between them.

Write S for summer clothes, W for winter clothes and R for rainy season clothes.

The Food We Eat

Listen to the story of Hari and Asha.

1

2

3

4

Read about the food we get from plants.

fruits

vegetables

nuts

rice

wheat

corn

Read about the food we get from animals.

eggs

cheese

milk

ghee

fish

Read about the food items we eat raw.

fruits

tomato

cucumber

nuts

carrot

Read about the food items we cook and eat.

egg

fish

potato

noodles

rice

okra

Tick (✓) the food items we get from plants.

Cross (✗) the food items that cannot be eaten raw.

Rana and Ronny

Look at the pictures. Listen to the story of Rana and Ronny.

1

2

3

4

5

Help Rana reach his plate full of healthy food!

Take all the healthy food items to the plate.

Different Tastes

Point and read.

sweet

sour

bitter

salty

spicy

Draw pictures of food items that have the given taste.

sweet	bitter

Plants

Read about the parts of a plant.

Match the parts of the plant to the picture.

root

leaf

stem

flower

Look at this picture. Talk about it.

seed seedling plant

Plants need air, water, and sunlight to grow.

Animals on the Farm

Say the names of the animals in this picture. Talk about them.

rooster
hen
cow

Animals in the Zoo

Say the names of the animals in this picture. Talk about them.

Match the animals to their faces.

Take the animals to their homes.

Animals in Water

Say the names of the animals in the picture. Talk about them.

Hey you little animals dancing in the sea,
How did you get such pretty colours, won't you tell me?

Animals at Home

Say the names of the animals. Talk about them.

cat

dog

hamster

parrot

fish

rabbit

Do you have a pet at home? Draw a picture of your pet.

Birds Around Us

Sing.

Hello, I'm Birdie!
The tree is my home.
Worms and fruits are my food.
Twitter-twitter! I sing a song
And play all day long.

Birds Around Us

Say the names of the birds in this picture. Talk about them.

Young Ones of Animals

Take the animals to their babies.

Touch the pictures. Say the names of the mothers and their babies.

cow – calf

horse – colt

goat – kid

lioness – cub

dog – pup

cat – kitten

hen – chick

sheep –lamb

Match the animals to their young ones.

Match the animals to their sounds.

Meow

Neigh

Bark

Roar

Bleat

Insects Around Us

Sing.

Ant

Butterfly

Crawl like an ant.
Buzz like a bee.
Flutter like a butterfly
Hop like a grasshopper.

Bee

Mosquito

Grasshopper

Housefly

Trace the homes of the insects. Colour and complete the picture.

Harmful Insects

Cross out (✗) the wrong things.

I Know!

Match the animals to their homes.

Paste the correct stickers.

Moo-Moo

Bark

Meow

Neigh

Cross (✗) the odd one out.

My Country

See the flag of India.

National Symbols

Touch the pictures. Talk about them.

flag

peacock

mango

lotus

tiger

emblem

Colour the flag of India correctly.

National Holidays

Gandhi Jayanti
2 October

Independence Day
15 August

Republic Day
26 January

Match correctly.

Gandhi Jayanti •		• 15 August
Republic Day •		• 2 October
Independence Day •		• 26 January

Ring the correct option.

26 August 26 January

15 August 26 December

2 January 2 October

Common Gadgets at Home

Point and read.

television

computer

mixer grinder

refrigerator

oven

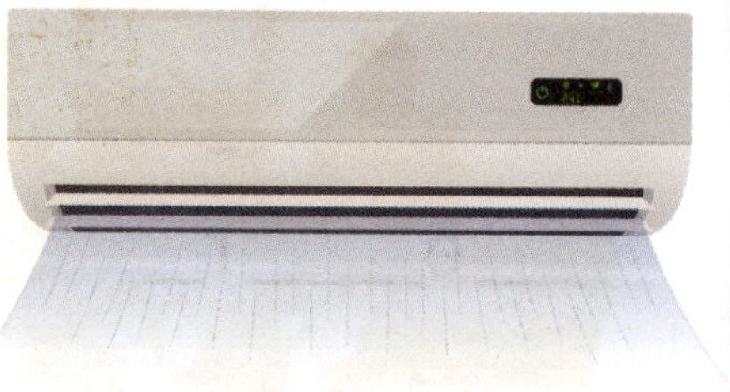

air conditioner

fan

clock

mobile

camera

Fill in the missing letters.

____el____v____s____o____

c____m____u____e____

____e____r____g____r____t____r

____ ____en

____an

lo

m il

Lily Likes

Listen to the story of Lily.

5

6

7

8

Tick (✔) the thing you like to do.

Colour the articles that you use at home.

Things Around Us

Look at the following pictures. Talk about them.

hard 

soft   

heavy   

light   

What happens when you put these in water? Tick (✓) the ones that float. Cross out (✗) the ones that sink.

objects	float	sink
 coin		
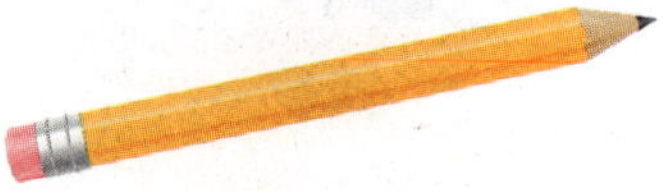 pencil		
 cotton ball		
 crayon		
 rubber band		
 wooden stick		

Festivals and Celebrations

Point and read.

Diwali

Christmas

Holi

Eid

Gurpurab

Colour the gifts.

Draw an X-mas tree.

Draw and colour a lamp.

Draw and colour two things you use to play Holi.

Means of Transport

Name the pictures. Talk about the pictures.

road

bus

cycle

car

water

ship

boat

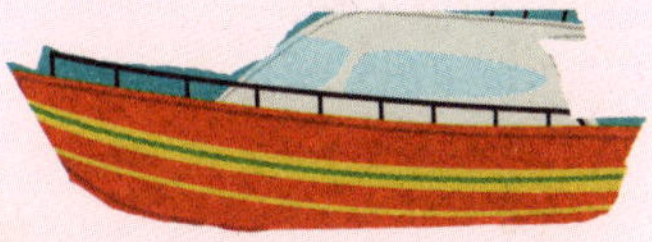
yacht

sky

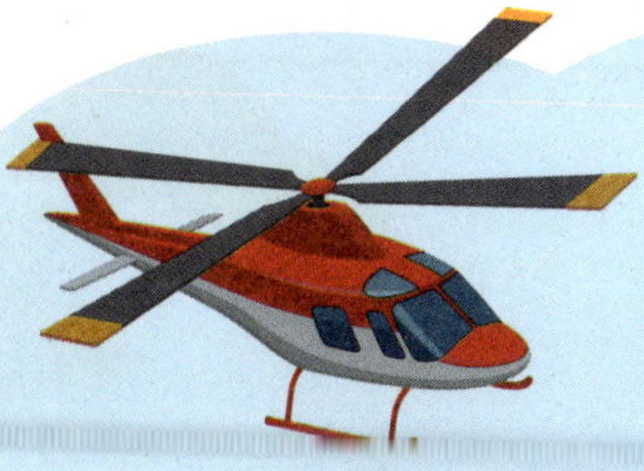
helicopter

aeroplane

hot air balloon

Paste the correct stickers.

Write the names of the given means of transport.

Benji Goes to the Market

Look at the pictures. Listen to the story of Benji.

1

2

3

4

5

6

Draw 2 things you like to buy from the market.

Point and read.

Clothes Shop
Bookshop
clothes
books
Vegetable Shop
Shoe Shop
fruits
vegetables
shoes

Ring the shops in the marketplace.

Tick (✓) the items you can buy from the market.

Games and Sports

Look at these pictures. Have you played any of these games?

ludo

carrom board

chess

hopscotch

cricket

hockey

Paste stickers of games in the correct place.

Indoor Games

Outdoor Games

Months of the Year

Listen to the story of 12 brothers.

1

2

3

4

5

Point and read.

January February March

April May June

July August September

October November December

Trace and write the names of the months.

January

February

March

April

May

June

July

August

September

October

November

December

Months of the Year

Paste stickers to show the missing months of the year.

I Am Ready

Sing.

I am bigger, I am stronger.
I am taller, I am sharper.
I know my letters and my manners.
I know the greetings and all the numbers.
I know about animals in land, air and water.
I know all about the people who help us.
I know how to keep safe at school, home and play.
I know that the traffic lights I must obey.
I am smarter now, smarter than before.
I am ready to move on, to learn some more.

Write your name here.

____

____

I am ____________ years old.

Paste your picture here.

Page 90:

Page 94:

February

March

April

May

July

September

November

Sticker page

Page 31:

Page 66:

Page 82: